*Adri*
*Thank you*
*for the*
*Support xoxo*
*Jess*

# Somewhere in the

# Middle

# Somewhere in the Middle

## Middle

Written by

## Jessica Gipson

For everyone that encouraged me to take my writing further, I love you all more than you know.

# Introduction

I fell in love with words at a very young age. Around that same age I learned that my voice, my thoughts, my feelings meant nothing; except on paper. My biggest dream is and will always be that someone finds them, my words, important and beautiful enough to read. In this crazy world, my words take me to a place that make sense. People talk about how books take them to another place, I hope my book does the same. I don't focus on rules of poetry I just let my pen guide me praying that someone can read and relate. My poetry is my alter ego. Real life has made me jaded, guarded and rough around the edges. My heart is a little smaller my mind is a little more closed. My writing however, is where I am open, I speak with and through my heart, I am vulnerable which is why it took me a long time to share my work. Slowly but surely I opened myself up to the people closest to me until I had enough courage to share myself with the world.

I thank the person reading this book in advance for letting me give you a tour through my mind and heart. Watch out for the broken pieces and don't be afraid of the dark.

# *Somewhere in the Middle*

I'm not black, I'm not white

I'm not the best, I'm not the worst

I'm not the favorite, I'm not the least

I'm where every part of me meets.

I'm not all love, nor pain

I'm not all survival or defeat

I'm not all rhyme or riddle

No matter what it is

I'm always somewhere in the middle.

# A Mother's Wisdom

Use me as your guiding light

To figure out what's wrong and right

I made enough mistakes for you both

Know everything I did was for

Your benefit and nothing more

It's been my blessing to watching you grow

Always remember to keep your word

Do what makes you happy

Just don't hurt the people you love and love you

Say please and thank you

Do what's right

Don't take no mess

But still be nice

Smile at the people who pass you by

Don't hold grudges

Don't seek revenge

Don't change who you are to make friends

Do as many good deeds as you can in a day

Don't boast your blessings or expect to lose them

Keep an open mind and don't judge

Protect each other

Do what you love

Remember I'm always here when you need

The world owes you no favors

So stand on your own two feet

You have two ears and one mouth

So listen more than you speak

Be aware of your surroundings

Use your sense

Say what you mean

Do what you meant

Don't be too stubborn to apologize

Always look others in the eyes

Don't say I love you unless you mean it

If you make a mess, be sure to clean it

Lead by example

Be a good friend

Keep the lies to a minimum

Treat people how you wish to be treated

Not how they treat you

Karma has a job

And so do you

Just a few lessons I tried to instill

Remember I love you and always will.

# Let's Go

Let's go to a block party

See a movie

Crash a wedding

Perhaps even go to our own

Let's go to Vegas

Or a museum

Or to a pond to cast stones

Let's go to church

Or to bed

Let's go write our names

In the stars

Let's go to heaven

Or karaoke

Let's go home

Or somewhere far

Let's go get ice cream

Or make a baby

On a Sunday afternoon

Let's go on a picnic

Or a safari

Let's go dive beneath the sea

Let's go dancing

Or to France

Let's go hear some poetry

Let's go nowhere

Or to the moon

Let's go to forever

Follow me.

# The Affair

You kissed me goodbye

As you put your ring back on

I acted as if I regretted the affair

But only so you don't collect to many sins

The next life won't be as beautiful

If you're not there

# *Words*

I'll love you

You have my word

All of my words

And I'll love you in their quantity


Just love me

Give me your word

All of your words

And love me in their quality

# *Your Story*

You found me on the shelf
lost among the many.
You picked me up,
dusted me off,
opened me up, ever so gently
and you read me
became lost in me.
Now, I am your story.

# *I Love You*

So many words

So few lines to write

So behind silent lips

And screaming thoughts

I hide.

I can't seem to come clean

Of all that is inside of me

If only you could part my mind

The way you have my thighs

And reveal words unuttered

You leave me, never hearing

The many times I muttered

I love you.

# *Easy*

You are my everything

That should have been

And everything

That may never be.

Somewhere between

My soulmate

And the one that got away.

I loved you once with the warmth

Of a summer breeze

And lost you just as easily.

# *Exposed*

I feel naked

Without my pride

I feel naked

Without my lies

Now I am here

Exposed

So tell me what it is

In these tears

I'm going to drown

In this silence

It's so loud

But I'm here

Exposed

So tell me what it is

Before my pride finds me

Like my shadow

And drags me back to the shallow

Take my hand

Jump in the deep with me

I owe you more than painful memories

Where you can't stand

To even think of me

So I'm here

Exposed

Tell me what it is.


He looked at me

With empty eyes

Only the darkness

I left inside.

He turned and left

And without speaking

He told me what it is.

# Let Go

These aren't tears of sadness because you left.

These are tears of triumph that I finally let go.

# *Procrastinator*

I clutch

So many "buts"

So many "if onlys", "maybes" and "possiblys"

Holding out hope for possibilities

No guarantee, just possibly

Never right now, for sure, definitely

I keep a little wiggle room

In all of my commitments

Can't commit, shit.

The next best thing is always on the way

Always tomorrow

Never today

Tons of "one days"

Even more "laters"

Welcome to the life of a procrastinator.

# *Lust*

He got me thinking things

Not fit for a Christian

Men like that

Make you lose your religion.

# *Lesson*

He wasn't meant for a forever

He wasn't supposed to be a victory

He was only meant to be a blessing

He was intended to be a teacher

And I learned my lesson.

# Despite

Despite every wrong

Every broken promise

Despite every lie

And my heart being broken

I still love that man


Despite every tear

And every reason to cry them

Despite all the years

I had to live without him

I still love that man


Don't ask me why

I have no answer

He's killing me

My own form of cancer

But I still love that man

# Misunderstanding

It was written in the stars

For us to meet

For us to love

For us to leave

Who ever said forever?

# *Beautiful Lies*

See, I'm in love with words.

Probably more than I was ever in love with him.

He had a way with words,

Which allowed him to have his way with me.

He lies so beautifully.

# Simple

I just want a bed with lots of pillows

To say I've felt sand between my toes

To let snow melt on my tongue

And hear rain on window panes

Simple girl

Simple things

Collar bone caresses

Forehead kisses

Movie nights and party dresses

In my closet

Skeletons, but more shoes

Simple girl

Simple rules

To hear my children's laughter

And their children's too

Spring air and lazy afternoons

Hot showers and relaxing baths

Good wine and candlelight

Simple girl

Simple rights

Fights but only with makeups

Lessons learned after every break up

Music and poetry

Lots of laughs

Fewer tears

Simple girl

Simple prayers

Good health

Modest wealth

Delicious food

And books on shelves

Family and friends

Humility and captured dreams

What's left?

Simple girl

Simple death.

# Say Grace

Devour me

Just say your grace first

# Believe

How can I believe heaven is a good place

when it keeps taking everyone I love?

# Fate

We were what we were

Until we weren't anymore.

We were what we were

For all the reasons we were for.

For all the love shared

And lessons learned

And not a reason more.

# Angel

Wait for me

At the edge of forever

I shall be there soon

Until I can see you again

Watch me from the moon.

# Perfect Imperfection

I'm not as soft as rose petals

nor sweet as fruit

My smooth surface

Hard to keep

It's burned deep

I'll always prefer black over pink

I can be mean

My mouth is real slick

Even if I bother wearing it

My nail polish will chip

I'm not for grand gestures

or PDA

So don't get upset when you reach for my hand

And I pull it away

I'll cry at movies

Pretend you don't see

I'm smarter than I look

But not as tough as I pretend to be

I use my humor as a shield

It protects me

I don't like hugs or pity

Just laugh with me

I'm not a hopeless romantic

In fact, I'm the opposite

I'll always wait for the other shoe to fall

Just make sure it doesn't

I'll support you

I'll encourage you

And give you words that are wise

I'll be your fan

I won't be fanatic

I'll be happy

But I'll never be ecstatic

I won't give up an easy apology

But I'll always make it right

I'm rough around the edges

and a little guarded

That tends to happen to

The abandoned and broken hearted

Everything I'm not

I'll make up for with everything I am

Even with all my flaws

I'll be perfect for the perfect man.

# Why?

Why give people second chances?

Death doesn't and that's who we are all living for.

# Heavenly

I just want to sit in the still

Bask in peace and calm

Blanketed by night sky

With nothing but ocean water

And star lights at my feet.

Glow with the moon

Dreading the sun

That will come too soon

I want happiness to fall from high

Like warm rain

And soak me with splendor

I am of the heavens

And to this world

I won't surrender.

# Vicious Cycle

I begged

I pleaded

At your silent request

I receded

I waited

Until I couldn't

I finally set my heart free

Someone found it

Cherished it

Then you came back to me.

# *Serial Killer*

She made a habit of leaving them

right after they couldn't live without her.

# *Fear*

I like you

But I'm scared to say that

I'm scared to feel that

I might not mean that

It might not be real yet

But how will I know that

If I don't put my faith down and leap it

I have butterflies in my stomach

Sweat in my palms

Lump in my throat

Evidence of my qualms

See, love hasn't been that easy on me

Or easy for me

And who knows the damage left on you

From those before me

So I'll watch you from here

From the shadows

Maybe in the still

You'll hear my thoughts

Maybe in a stolen gaze

You'll see the intent of my ways

I'm here

I like you

But not more than I fear you.

# *Where My Pain Lives*

He put my fingertips against his lips

and gently kissed them.

He said he knows where my pain is

and this is where my pain lives.

# *I'm a Drug*

If I make you fall in love,

I'll be your addiction.

I'll be the cause and cure

To all your afflictions.

# The Poet

She wrote few words,

and the few she did, simple.

Yet they were the ink of my complex heart.

Poem after poem,

be it just a line,

was a memory of mine

She was the narrator

of my own diary.

A stranger, continents away,

knew me so thoroughly.

# *Before He Leaves*

If I wake up early enough,

I can catch a glimpse of him before he leaves,

and I get to

Taste the kiss he leaves on me.

# *Magic*

We made love

On a stormy night

Our noise mixed with thunder

In the dark

Our bodies entangled

Intertwined together

Once in a while

The lightening would flash

And I would get to witness magic

# Ruin Me

Hours of precision

To sour eyes, I'm a vision

You can tell I took my time

A little perfume

A little lace

Gently placed on silk sheets

Now tear it all apart

And ruin me

# *Remember When*

Remember when time had no meaning?

We would talk for hours without meaning.

Remember when it was simple

and laughter came with ease?

Remember when?

And if you don't,

may I remind you please?

Remember these lips,

like silk, you said, against your skin?

Remember this dimple?

It was your favorite then.

Remember this shape

your fingers would trace and outline?

Remember your hands

and how they felt in mine?

Remember these legs

and how they would part and get tangled up in yours?

Remember these inner thighs

resting like the sea shore?

Remember this collar bone and nape

and the kisses you would give?

I'll let you in to remember more

Just don't forget again.

# Days of Daze

In our days of love

We were in a daze of love

We didn't even see the ending coming

# Dreams & Love

She had a dream

Bigger than a dream should be.

So big,

it's what made her breathe.

But she had a love,

Stronger than a love should be.

And her strength was in her ability

to hold onto both tightly

Living both equally.

# *Poetically in Tune*

I am poetically in tune with all that inspires

Words run through me like the blood in veins

I write

I scribe

Jot down

And type

Songs with no sweet voice or music in the way

Poetry will be my passion

Until I wither away

And even then I'll live forever

Among the pages that I shared

Read any of my lines

And you will find me there

# *Love is Forever*

I want to love you with the power of a million forevers.

Intensely.

And though we won't live long enough to see

the full magnitude of it,

Light years will carry us on.

# *Jaded View*

A piece of paper

A piece of metal

And a sinner's vow to God,

What is it worth today?

Forever is getting shorter.

Pretty soon it won't exist.

But they say that's why we exist

To accomplish this.

So I aspire,

with the right attitude and proper attire,

I'll inspire

Someone to bend his knee

Promise a tomorrow

That is not even promised to me.

In a society of smoke and mirrors

I'm supposed to expect this to be real.

So I'll take his ring,

worth three times his salary,

and pretend to be a virgin for a day.

Pay money to entertain naysayers

who smile in my face.

Make a promise to the preacher man

we may not keep.

See, it's not so hard to share

A piece of paper

A piece of metal

And a sinner's vow to God.

# *Phoenix*

You have to be burned

To rise from the ashes

# His Story

Everyone knows a woman's pain

How she was broken, hurt and unprotected.

But a man's game

Is simply expected and the why is rejected.

But *this* man

Spilled his guts and put them in his dutch

Rolls up and fades away.

He goes on and on like Badu's song

And I

I get to listen

To stories about dead friends,

His deadbeat dad and the effects crack had.

How he got everyone high just to keep his mom from

The first time he had to use his gun

On his best friend.

This was back then, back when

His true love told real lies

And he didn't realize

Until his first born didn't have his eyes

And I

I get to listen.

My attention is captured

By stories that lack rapture

Time freezes in a smoky haze

As he reminisces of gold chains and new Jays

And the shoe box that held his glory

But his black queen was a crack fiend

So it was gone by the morning.

He inhales

And laughs at and about dumb shit

Like 13 inch rims and throwbacks.

If only he could go back and find me there

How different life would be.

He has to get high just to trust me

And never high enough to love me.

But I,

I get to listen.

That is my position and I play it well

On the floor before him I dwell.

I just listen.

And as the smoke dissipates

So do we

Him with my heart

And I with his story.

# *Princess–ish*

Me, a princess hardly

But I still seek a prince charming

Not to rescue me from my tower with a kiss

But one I slay dragons with.

# *Ailment*

Love is in the air

I know better than to breathe it in

I don't ever

Ever want to be love sick again

# *You Were*

You were so perfect

You were so worth it

You made me forget

My heart was hurting

You were so precious

You were so fine

And above all else

You were all mine

# *My Life*

Life is a white room

with polar bear rugs and fine china.

And I came through like a tornado

with mud on my boots and paint on my fingers.

# *Your Lies*

Your lies kept me smiling.

Your lies kept me blinded.

I was the happiest I'd ever been

when you were lying to me.

Now I'm stuck in the darkness.

Trapped in this despair.

But they say

The truth sets you free.

# I Knew Him When

Pained, to see a broken man

Disdained, because I broke that man

He can't leave his mark on the world

Because I left a scar on his heart

At night, I fall to my knees

Before I thank God for my blessings

I pray for his peace

For his hurt to cease

Or at the very least

Decrease

I know I'm flawed

And was more so then

At least I can say

I knew him when

# Dead Butterflies

At every glance, touch, or hello

You gave me butterflies.

And after every cheat, tear, lie,

I still felt the butterflies.

Then you forced me to say goodbye.

It wasn't until our next hello that I realized

All my butterflies had died.

# Obstacle

The only thing harder than getting into a heart you didn't
break

Is getting back into the one you did.

# *Beware*

You won't feel the fall

Or be aware of the drop

But one day, I'll just appear

Like steam from a shower that's too hot

# The Privileged

You kill a Morehouse man.

You outlawed the Black Panthers.

No matter what I do,

my skin will still be black, sir.

Even if I bleach it,

my kin will still be black sir.

What would you have me do?

Get in a field and pick some cotton for you?

Get on a field and run a tackle for you?

Hop on a track and quote a rap lyric or two?

No matter what I do,

you'll still think I belong to you.

That's why you're okay

with killing a black or two.

# Love's Contradiction

We all have a dream to live a love

that is pure and everlasting

But the love stories that make history

are full of loss and tragedy

# *Audacity*

I set fire to the

Petals of dandelions

and still have the audacity

to expect my wishes to come true.

# Outside Influence

You like to listen to

He said, she said

But stick together is what we said

Forever, 'til we dead

You're letting the devil get the best of you

Then coming home

And giving me the rest of you

# *Blessing*

I thank God for tragedy

So I can fully appreciate

Something as beautiful as this

# Will Power

It's been a while

It's been some time

Since someone stroked my spine

Or kissed my panty line

All my power willed

To keep dressed

As our lips pressed

And I'm gently caressed

Soft music

Moonlight

Rain drops

And a cool breeze

With ease this came

Pressure on my frame

All my power willed

To maintain my composure

Had to end it

Though I didn't want it over

I rolled over

He left traces of kisses

From my nape to my hips

I felt his love

It poured on thick

But I made it out

Safe and sound

In this pool of lust

I almost drowned

All my power willed

To calm down

I saved face

With my self-respect

And stained grace

Now I lay here alone and dazed

Lost in daydreams still

But all my power willed

# Hope & Despair

I have the death grip on light and hope.

When I let go,

into the darkness I float.

That's worse than drowning you know.

# Losing Him

To lose him meant to feel

the pain from everything that happened,

and that of everything

that never will.

# *What If*

The chemistry was there between subtle stares and flirty caper. Conversation tread from light to heavy with such ease. A future in the midst, but steps not taken because of bad timing and circumstance. I wonder if we had parted lips before we parted ways, would that have been our last goodbye? As what ifs dance circles in my mind, no time was given, so time won't tell. Oh well, lives go on and hearts beat more, drumming out the few memories we had stored. Now and then, a reminisce will glaze our minds and pass by, as freely as wind in the sky.

# *Coy*

You say hello. Butterflies flutter. I utter the same in reply, bat my eyes and flash a smile. I walk away and let my hip sway, like trees in the breeze. If only each meeting were as sweet and coy as this.

# I Wish

I wish I loved him like I loved words

Lyrically he's my soul mate

Really he's my enemy

I wish I could meet him on a notepad

I'd let him write scriptures on my spine

And we could reproduce rhyme

# *Past Tense*

You used to be my everything

Now you're everything but

# *You Can*

You can stop me

You can tell me not to cry

You can wipe away my tears

And tell me everything will be alright

But you're not here to stop me

You're not here to tell me not to cry

You're not here to wipe away my tears

And tell me everything will be alright

And that's the reason I'm crying in the first place.

# *Poetry*

It was like poetry

Sweet, sweet poetry

Except no words were spoken

You were just holding me

# *Pieces*

Come to me with the pieces of your broken heart

And I'll come to you with mine

All the pain that broke our hearts was perfect, see

Our pieces fit together perfectly.

# Stroking Egos

Once lovers

Now friends

Only because you think

You can have me on a whim

Oh darling, try

You think you can

I'd ask that you think again

# *Love Me*

Love me tender

Love me sweet

Love me kindly

Love me deep

Love me forever

And more than enough

Love me when it's easy

Love me when it's rough

Love me uncontrollably

Love me with ease

Love me now

Or tomorrow

Just love me

Please

# Limits of Desperation

My knees will bend to pray for you to stay,

but never to beg.

# *Take A Piece*

Our love has died.

It is time to make peace with it.

But please, take a piece of it,

as a reminder, one time we got it right.

# Rebound

You were a fleeting moment

in the absence of love.

But somewhere along the way,

I got confused.

I convinced myself that I found love.

I convinced myself it was you.

# Falling

Slowly

Deeply

Falling

Wearing nothing but moonlight

My skin lost among yours

The wind that blows in

Reminds us that there is a world out there

We soon forget again

Surely

Sweetly

Falling

Bathing in darkness

My lips lost between yours

The sunshine reminds us a new day has come

Yet we forget again

Intensely

Definitely

Falling

# *Prayer*

As I lay me down to sleep,

I pray the Lord that I not weep

over love or friendships lost.

It pays to grow

and they the cost.

As I lay me down to rest,

friend or foe

I pray you're bless

# Superhero

There is magic between these lips

I can breathe life into you

Or I can suck it out

Shatter doubt with sweet lies

Or sweeter truths

There is power between these hips

Here lies your weakness

And your strength

Your future

And your youth

I conquer all with delicate hands

And soft skin

This harsh world has no effect

So man, don't question my ability

To handle all I endure

My sex is my superpower

What's yours?

# *Dead Flower*

He's a dead flower.

But I continue to water him,

convinced that he will grow.

# He Touched Me

He touched me and I felt love

He touched me and I felt spiritual

He touched me and I felt his soul

I felt growing old

And memories unmet

He touched me and he felt skin

He touched me and felt lustful sin

He touched me and thought

He'd never touch me again

He thought finally and on to the next

Good thing I thought this through

And I won't let him touch me yet

# Behind The Pen

Behind the pen,

I can make believe I'm behind the camera.

Make pictures, take pictures,

Write.

Behind the pen,

I can pretend I'm behind the mic.

Make music, lovely music

Write.

Behind the pen,

I can fight the good fight

and win, and again,

Write.

Behind the pen,

I can imagine I'm under him.

Make love, not war

Write.

Behind the pen,

there is no hiding.

It's the key to all doors.

Let me open yours.

Write.

Behind the pen,

like behind the alter, I give explanations

to the congregations, heavenly

Write.

Behind the pen,

I stand tall behind the law.

It's my right to write

Right?

Behind the pen,

I can explain decisions and express convictions,

romance with good diction.

My reasons to write come in plethoras,

and live past etceteras.

I give pieces of me

with every word I leave.

That is why

I write.

# Cages

She loved a man

who loved her unconditionally.

Every one of her flaws,

even those that were cause to his broken heart.

She loved a man,

until she realized she didn't.

His love had conditions,

but she had been conditioned.

She was a free bird

and he was shopping for cages.

# *You Lie*

you lie about where you are

you lie about who you're with

you lie about simple things like what time it is

but when you say "I love you"

you expect me to believe you

# *Warn Them*

Bad girls never been good to you

Good girls never been good enough

At least warn the women who chase you

Not to cut their feet

On the trail of the broken hearts you leave behind

# My Heart

I used to wear my heart on my sleeve,

like a fancy button.

But somewhere along the way,

I lost it.

.

# *Love Was Never*

# *Enough*

I'm not good at this love thing

But I tried anyway

You sought something I didn't have

But I tried anyway

Until one day you found love among a pack of
wolves

with their teeth shining

ha, you thought they were smiling

I watched you get devoured

And no amount of my love

Could have stopped it

# No Swimming Allowed

You enticed me with your warmth

You were calm and gentle

While I dipped my feet in

You loved me with your depth

Once you had my body

You surrounded me

You fooled me with your beauty

Your soothing waves pulled in further

And took me under

It became harder to keep my head above water

By dawn I was swept to shore

# Lost in Wonder

When I leave, the clues will be far and few between.

You'll remember my smile and the corky way I
laughed.

You'll remember my strength

and all the things in which I took a stand.

You'll remember my love,

and my methods of doing so.

But after you set the memories aside,

you'll be riddled with the why

and you won't find comfort in knowing

So was I.

# Tainted Memories

I began to miss you many years ago

while you were still by my side.

I was just too stubborn to speak up.

I began losing you all that time ago,

when your hand would still hold mine.

I was just too cowardly to give up.

Now I'm left with the rubble of memories

that an earthquake of pain left behind,

and even if I could put them back together

what would they be worth?

# Naïve

In life, you only get so many beautiful moments

where you can be blissfully naïve…

…I wasted all of mine on you.

# Soul Mate

Before my eyes caught your glance

Before you walked in my direction

Before you extended your hand, and gave an
introduction

I recognized you

# Idealistic

She was a beautiful artist.

In every person she met,

she carved her words

and painted a memory.

# Recipe for Disaster

I had composure, confidence and will power,

I had pride, ego and some class.

The sugar and spices of a lady.

Until you set a fire and brought it to a boil,

and sprinkled in a dash of you.

Who knew

that was the recipe for disaster?

# *Pillow Talk*

How soon you forget

I was on that pillow with you.

How soon you'll remember

I know secrets, too.

# *In My Eyes*

In my eyes

You were undefeatable

In my eyes

You were king

In my eyes

You had no flaws

In my eyes

You were everything

Then you drank poison

It sizzled on your tongue

You saw fit to lie to me

While staring

In my eyes

# *Dear John*

You don't see your wrongs.

You don't see your faults.

How can I get you to see the error of your ways

if you think everything is okay?

This is normal for you

and nothing will change.

So I can't stay.

# *Silence*

Stop.

Take a moment to listen.

All of the answers to the questions you have

can be found in my silence.

# On Purpose

With all the accidents and mistakes

that take place,

I chose to love you on purpose.

Remember that.

# *Ordinary*

I held you to a standard

as high as the star I wished on to get you,

and then one day I woke up,

and you were ordinary.

# *Cursed*

You're cursed with me

Your thought may linger

And become faint

But still, I'll be a constant reminder

Of the chance you didn't take

# *Divine Flaws*

To err is human

To forgive is divine

So please forgive all of these divine flaws of mine

They're perfectly fitted

I'm just a sin

Waiting to be committed

# Perfection

You want me to be

the girl of your dreams.

What you see on TV.

What you see on IG.

I ask that you join me in the real world, dear friend.

I am as close to perfect as you're going to get.

# *Coping*

You got to love me intensely

Hurt me immensely

Shatter my heart

And use the pieces as something borrowed on your
wedding day

I'm just trying to pretend I have it all together

# *Favored Memory*

When I laid my eyes

to rest on yours,

I knew in that moment

it would be a favored memory.

# Old World Order

Did you know it's illegal

to kidnap, rape, and sell human beings?

Kill, defile, and enslave human beings?

Hang, set fire to, and rename human beings?

But when the laws are red, white and blue,

they're so flexible.

This land was built with slaves and masters,

and though there is a black man

in The White House

with a mantra for change,

not much has.

# *Perfect Vacation*

I just want sex that's good for me

Food that's bad for me

And a man to love me for the days

Good weather for the weekend

Warm sand to sink my feet in

And a sweet martini in my hand

Girlfriends up for a good time

Memories to last a lifetime

And a home that misses me while I'm gone

# *Bad Apple*

I wasn't a bad apple

until you sunk your teeth into me.

# The Pact

Remember that day we made a pact to give up on
each other?

Me either.

# *Kind of Love*

I want the kind of love

that seems to only exist

in music notes and on silver screens.

I want it to be rare, extraordinary

over exaggerated, yet real.

# Common Features

You and time have something in common.

You both make me think I have more of you

than I actually do.

# *Unable*

I had a hole in my soul

You had a hole in yours

Neither of us could fill the other's

# Future Husband

Tie your words into a noose

Let me hang from it

My eardrums are your instrument

Let your voice bang on them

My shoulders can bear the weight

Whenever you need to lean

I am here until I'm gone

There is no in between

My virtues all exist for you

I was handpicked, created, designed

From your side, so I can stand there

Let me take my place

For you and all you bring I'll surrender my name

I was nothing but in pieces until you came

You make me whole

Together we are one

I will love you unconditionally

Whole heartedly

Until God sets my sun

# I Stayed

I stayed out of guilt

I stayed out of comfort

I stayed out of complacency

I stayed out of habit

I stayed for the kids

I stayed for the time invested

But I never considered staying for love

Or I would have left sooner

# *Regret*

Full of liquor, loneliness

and the urge to make decisions.

I'm in no condition to love you tonight,

but I will anyway.

Regret will come in the morning

# *Detached*

Some of my friends

have become perfect strangers,

some great loves.

Nothing but faded memories,

I am learning to nod my head and smile,

maybe even laugh.

But for my heart's sake,

I do not get too attached.

# *Strength*

Every heartbreak

Every mistake

Every mishap

Every setback

Every first kiss

Every last

Every forced smile

Every tear cried

Every bended knee

Every prayer sent

Has prepared me for this moment

# *Acrophobia*

I want to say I love you

But I keep it to goodnight

Love involves some falling

And I'm afraid of heights

# *Time*

Time is like the tide

with its constant movements.

It's always either pushing people closer

or pulling them away.

# Mixed Up

House Nigger.

Like I was better than the slaves,

like I liked the fact

that my mother was stolen

from her husband and raped.


I am a mix between the colored

hanging from a tree with a rope

around his neck,

and the Klan that put it there

in the first place.


Growing up innocent,

not knowing.

Wondering why I was turned away

from white circles,

and why my black family

looked at me differently.


I got laughed at

by even my grandest of parents.

I hated everyone.

I hated my father for sleeping

with that honkey bitch.

And my mother for letting

that nigger in her bed.

I hated myself for not being

able to accept myself.


I was mad I couldn't wear weave

and get perms.

I was mad my ass and hips

were too big to fit in

Abercrombie and Fitch.

I was mad that I didn't know

what box to check...black, white, other?

So I checked all three, shit.... Y'all think I had it easy

because my skin is fair

and my hair is long.

I grew up not knowing where

I belonged.


Feeling uneasy learning

about history

'cause I felt I had no history.

Feeling my whole existence

was a mystery.


Terms like

mixed, biracial and mullato,

all foreign to me.

I grew up hearing mut

and half breed,

like I was a genetic mistake.

Do you know how it feels

to be misplaced?

Not classed in any race?


Black friends would make "White Jokes"

like I wasn't one of them.

I was mixed up and

what's fucked up

is that I taught myself

how to deal,

and I am still learning.


But I don't know

if I am learning to be

more accepting or

creating my own racism.

.... God Bless me

# *Beautiful Pain*

Being hurt by the love of my life

is the most beautiful pain I have ever felt.

# *Impossible*

Whoever said

Love makes all things possible

was spreading lies.

Because this love of ours is impossible,

no matter how we try.

# Love and Pain

Love is simply

giving one the power

to hurt you,

while hoping that they won't.

Pain is that hope

leading you astray,

and the one you love

using the power you gave.

# *Plenty of Fish*

Plenty of fish in the sea, they say.

I say, plenty of sharks, too.

And they'll eat you alive.

# *Beautiful*

Beauty is in the eye of the beholder

So behold me

Or just hold me

That makes me feel beautiful too

# My Ghost

You are a ghost of the man you used to be.

Your kiss, your scent, your touch,

everything you used to be.

And you haunt me.

# Pieces to Peace

I wasn't always this way.

Closed off and guarded,

Jaded and broken-hearted.

I recall

when I was young and naïve,

trust bursting out of my seams,

but every person I let near my heart

chipped away a piece.

So what I'm left with I protect it

I guard it with my life.

I can use it to find the light in all my darkness,

if I use it right.

As long as you can find love in your pieces

then a broken heart is not in vain.

# The Flaws of Stars

Stars have flaws, too.

Sometimes they grant the wrong wishes.

# Mystery of Love

The mystery of love

Is the mystery of magic

It could all be an illusion

It could all be a hat trick

Or it could be God

Juggling dimensions

Making the impossible form

Like she from he

Flesh from bones

I came from his ribs

To live in his soul

# *Saturday Night*

It's Saturday night

Kiss me like

Sunday morning doesn't exist

# *Sinful*

I've committed a sin

and been forgiven.

But if given the chance,

I'll commit it again.

# Same Page

I said,

I'm falling

I'm falling

Catch me when I do

He replied,

I can't

I'm falling, too

# *Taste of Pain*

As soon as his lips

pressed against hers,

He tasted every tear that she cried,

and every year that she hurt.

In that moment He knew

He'd never fully have her.

She was a chained slave

and pain was her master.

# *Where Unicorns Live*

Kept promises

True love

Loyalty and honesty

Must only exist

Where unicorns live

# *Misled*

Whoever said, "follow your heart"

was never led to you.

# Dandelion

Even with the thorns,

She was no rose.

She was tougher,

more resilient.

She was a pop of color

in a world of darkness,

without even trying.

She was better known

as a dandelion.

# A Smile

She sees rejection

She sees abandonment

She sees rape, abuse and lack of commitment

She sees average, unworthy, not worth the while

But the world sees

A smile

Strength and conviction

But what the world sees is fiction

A smile is never the true you

A smile can fool you

# Gone Astray

I watched him stray from who he was

To everything he said he'd never be

I watched him wander to a place

He said he'd never go

Apart of my flesh became someone I didn't know

He tried to jump off the edge holding my hand

But I knew I had to let go

# I Bleed Words

I bleed words.

Slice me open and leave me

in a pool of poetry.

# *One Wish Away*

Outside my window is a star

When I look out my window

There you are

You're only one wish away

# *Mortal*

He was strength

when I was weak.

With him I was invincible,

like I could take over the world.

He made me forget, if only for moments,

that I was mortal.

# *Line by Line*

Open me up

Read what is inside

Line by line

Until you have me memorized.

# One Night Stand

If these sheets could talk,

they would be too ashamed to.

Please don't fall in love with me,

but if so, I don't blame you.

Kiss me goodbye now,

because I'll be gone by the morning.

# Hiding Place

When he was alone and afraid

I was his favorite hiding place

# *Hindsight*

Whether the start of something horrible,

or the end of something beautiful,

You won't know until it's too late.

# *My Beauty*

My beauty lies in the wars I've won

Not the battles I've lost

My beauty lies in everything I am

Not in everything I'm not

You can find me in the darkest secrets

Shining my brightest light

My beauty is found in my flaws

Even when I'm not right

# Come and Go

You come and go

Just to cum and go

Next time you come

You'll find a locked door

That leads to a heart

That doesn't love you anymore

# Sin and Love

Sin never tasted as good

as when I kissed him.

Love never felt so bad

as when I missed him.

# *My Words*

I write so my words

migrate to you like swallows to warmer weather.

I hope they take over you like the sky

and find you fit to call them home for a while.

# *Too Busy*

I'm at a loss for words

When I'm too busy loving them

I'm at a loss for love

When I'm too busy writing about it

# The Parallel

Love and pain are parallel

That's why we hurt the ones we love the most

Love and pain are like heaven and hell

So far, yet so incredibly close

So honey, let me kiss the scars I've inflicted

And let our burdens go

# I Watch Them

I watch them

Live, laugh, and love

I watch them

Find their soul mates and loves of their lives

I find solace thinking

I had a part in it

I was a part of it

I watch them alone

And I'm living my karma

# Beautiful Destination

I, myself, am a journey

Please embark

Look at my smile as the beginning

Kiss here to start

I can be a wild ride

So if you need to hold on tight

Here's my hand

Forever is a beautiful destination

You'll see for yourself when we land

.

# *Dead on Arrival*

I placed my mouth on your mouth

I placed my hands on your chest

I attempted to revive us

What was left

But I'm sad to pronounce

We're dead

# *Still Burning*

I loved you with a fire I thought would never burn
out.

And even now, laying with him, it smolders.

I don't think a love like that is meant to be felt twice

or done over.

# Do You?

Do you read my lines and know, without a shadow
of a doubt, they were written for you?

I'll never admit a thing

I'll just keep writing

I hope you keep reading

# I Won't Promise

I won't promise you a forever up front.

Every night before we fall asleep,

I'll kiss you goodnight,

and promise you a tomorrow.

# Russian Roulette

Maybe you love me

Maybe you don't

Stop playing Russian roulette

Love is never in the balance

It is or it isn't

So just open fire

And make it quick

My heart just might survive it

# *Heaven Called*

Heaven called

Your wings are ready

It's time for us to watch you fly

We have so many beautiful memories

Our eyes won't even let us cry

# *No Comparison*

Yes, I love you both

But I can't compare you two

Doing so is like comparing

The ocean to a swimming pool

# Favorite Song

It's all I want

After a day so long

I just want to lay on your chest

And listen to my favorite song

# One Night

One Night, last night

There was no resistance

There was only us

Alone in existence

There was no her, no him, no limit

We were so close

Holding each other so tight

Our complexions blended

The lights were off

But we could still look into each other's eyes

We were consumed by the darkness

Along with our passion for each other

There was no confusion, no awkwardness, no doubt

We were meant for each other

If only for one night, last night.

# Instrumental

My spine, his percussion

My waistline, his piano

He gave me music

I was his soprano

He gave me rhythm

He gave me blues

He gave me memories

I could hum to

I gave him my heart

So to him it belonged

But he used it as a bass

He kept stringing me along

And I kept singing along

Until one day

The melody faded

# My Choice

He asked,

"Do you want to be happy

Or

Do you want to be a writer?"

Not many are allowed to be both.

I picked up my pen, my notepad, and a bottle of whiskey.

I guess I made my choice.

Some call this an end

Others call it a beginning

Made in the USA
Charleston, SC
27 July 2016